HOW TO BUILD & MONITOR BUSINESS CREDIT

A Beginner's Guide to LLC Vendor Tradelines, High D&B Scores, and Becoming a Fundable Business Without Personal Risk

You Built an LLC.
Now Build the Credit to Match.

PANTHEON SPACE ACADEMY

HOW TO BUILD & MONITOR BUSINESS CREDIT
A Beginner's Guide to LLC Vendor Tradelines, High D&B Scores, and Becoming a Fundable Business Without Personal Risk

PANTHEON SPACE ACADEMY

Printed Worldwide
First Printing 2026
First Edition 2026

ISBN: 978-1-970965-00-1

10 9 8 7 6 5 4 3 2 1

LEGAL NOTICE

Disclaimer Notice:

Please note that the information contained within this document is for educational and entertainment purposes only. It does not guarantee any specific outcome, lender approval, or credit limit. Regulations, underwriting standards, and vendor policies change frequently; readers must verify all critical details directly with financial institutions, credit bureaus, and qualified advisors. Using this information does not create a client or fiduciary relationship. Your compliance with local, state, and federal regulations is your responsibility.

Every effort has been made to present accurate, up-to-date, and reliable, complete information. No warranties of any kind are declared or implied. Readers acknowledge that the author is not engaging in the rendering of legal, financial, medical, or professional advice. The content

TABLE OF CONTENTS

Introduction

Who This Book Is For

If you've recently formed an LLC — or you're in the early stages of building your business — this book was written for you.

Specifically, it's for small business owners in the United States who are ready to stop mixing personal and business finances, stop relying on personal credit to fund their company, and start building a legitimate business credit profile that stands on its own.

You don't need to be a financial expert. You don't need years of business history. You just need to be willing to follow a clear, step-by-step process — and do it the right way.

Whether you're a solo entrepreneur, a family business, or an early-stage company with big plans, this guide meets you exactly where you are.

What to Expect

This book is a practical roadmap — not theory, not hype, not a list of shortcuts that don't work.

By the time you finish this book, you'll understand:

- What No-PG business credit actually means and what it can realistically do for your LLC
- How to build and sequence your business profile step by step without touching your personal FICO score
- How long the process really takes and what friction points to expect along the way
- Why applications get denied, how D&B and other bureaus actually process your information, and how to verify your progress
- How to troubleshoot problems, fix reporting errors, and keep building even when obstacles appear

Every chapter is designed for beginners but is honest about the real complexity of U.S. business finance. No fluff. No filler. Just the information you need in the order you need it.

A Note on No-PG Pathways

Let's be honest about something upfront.

There are a lot of people online promising instant approvals, secret vendor lists, and guaranteed business credit cards with no personal guarantee. Avoid them. These promises are either misleading, outdated, or outright false — and following bad advice early in the process can set your business back months.

Building business credit the right way is not fast. It is not a secret. But it is absolutely achievable — and when you do it properly, the results are real, lasting, and genuinely valuable to your business.

This guide will show you exactly how. One step at a time.

Before you begin — your free digital worksheet is waiting.

The First 90 Days Compliance Checklist at the back of this book — after the ***Conclusion.*** It's also available as a free digital version. It's your step-by-step instructions to help you stay organized and prepared for your first 90 days. Download it, fill it in on any device, or print it on standard 8.5" x 11" paper and work through it by hand alongside the book.

Feel free to write inside this book, use the digital version, or print it on larger paper. We recommend printing it onto 8.5" x 11" paper for the best experience.

Scan the QR below or visit **pantheonspace.com/90daystocredit** and claim your free copy instantly.

Chapter 1

Foundation—Forming a Lender-Ready LLC

Building business credit that genuinely separates your business risk from your personal financial life starts with structure—how your LLC is formed, documented, and presented. This is far more than bureaucratic paperwork; it lays a path of credibility for every vendor, lender, or credit bureau interaction that follows.

Why This Foundation Matters

Credit bureaus and No-PG lenders operate in a world heavy with fraud, shell companies, and applicants seeking to "game" the system. Their first line of defense is basic due diligence: is this business *real*, is it structured in compliance with the law, and is it operated apart from the owner's finances? Establishing this "lender-ready" status signals you're legitimate and lowers the risk you'll trigger automated denials as a new applicant.

Action Guidance

Register Your LLC Properly

- File your Articles of Organization with your state's Secretary of State office, specifying your business name, address, registered agent, and ownership structure. Keep the official, filed copy in a safe place—it will be needed repeatedly.
- Maintain exact consistency in name and address formatting. For example, if your formation says "Main Street LLC," do not alternate between "Main Street, LLC," "Main Street Limited Liability Company," or other variants elsewhere.

Example:

Imagine you form "Mason Creek Logistics LLC" in Georgia, using your home address to file the paperwork. You later open a business checking account using "Mason Creek Logistics" (without the "LLC"), and another supplier lists you as "Mason Creek Logistics, LLC" at a virtual office. These variations—even a missing "LLC"—can result in a reporting mismatch and, in the worst cases, outright denials.

Obtain an EIN from the IRS

- An Employer Identification Number (EIN) is your business's unique tax ID. It's essential for tax filings, payroll, business bank account opening, and virtually any credit or vendor application.
- Apply only through the official IRS EIN portal—it's free, and approval is often immediate except in rare cases.
- Store your EIN confirmation notice safely; you'll usually be asked to upload or fax it to banks, vendors, or credit agencies on request.

Scenario:

After forming an LLC, a new owner delays applying for an EIN and tries to use their SSN to open bank accounts and set up Net 30 vendor accounts. Not only does this put their personal credit at risk, but it also guarantees nearly all "business credit" activities will be linked to their personal record—not the LLC.

Open a Dedicated Business Checking Account

- Separate accounts are crucial. Commingling funds—i.e., paying personal bills from business income or vice versa—risks your liability protections and credibility.
- Research banks in your area; not all are business-friendly, especially toward new entities or high-risk industries. Credit unions can offer more flexibility for smaller balances.
- You will typically be asked for your Articles of Organization, EIN, valid ID for all owners, a business license (if required locally), and sometimes verification of business address (such as a lease, utility bill, or website).

Common Edge Case:

Home-based businesses sometimes struggle to open accounts when the bank requires commercial lease documentation. In this case, consider a virtual office lease (from a provider with a solid reputation and physical location) or choose a bank that does not require a commercial lease for basic business industries.

Set Up a Physical Business Address and Phone Number

- Bureaus and lenders rely on business address and contact info to verify legitimacy. Registered agent or home addresses (especially apartments) can be flagged by automated systems.
- Consider a commercial mailing address (co-working or executive suite), but avoid "mailbox-only" stores like UPS, as many lenders have blacklisted these.
- Secure a dedicated business phone number, ideally listed in your LLC name (NOT your personal cell). VoIP lines (RingCentral, Grasshopper, etc.) work for most, but verify acceptance with key vendors.
- Purchase a business domain (e.g., www.masoncreeklogistics.com) and create a professional email (you@businessname.com).

Edge Case:

An e-commerce LLC that initially registered at the owner's apartment and later switched to a virtual office forgot to update its IRS and state records. Vendors cross-check addresses during credit application review, resulting in unexplained denials due to "address mismatch."

List Your Business with 411 Directory Assistance

- While less important than it was a decade ago, some legacy lenders and vendors still reference 411 public listings to verify your phone number and business existence.
- Services exist to register and maintain your business with 411; this can be skipped in some sectors, but for broad-appeal businesses (Ex, retail, light manufacturing), it's a helpful credibility signal.

Common Mistakes / Risk Awareness

- **Home Address Flags:** Commercial lenders and D&B may automatically flag applications submitted with a purely residential address or a mailbox-only suite.

- **Confused Communication Lines:** Using your cell number for both personal and business matters, or sharing a "catch-all" business line between entities, erodes separation.
- **License Gaps:** Some businesses do not require state licensing, but local municipalities might have requirements for sales tax, zoning, or industry-specific permits. Missing any of these can block account openings.

Troubleshooting / Recovery Guidance

Bank Denial Example:

Sherri, the new owner of a pet grooming LLC, is denied a business account because the bank says her documentation is incomplete. Upon review, she discovers that her EIN letter lists a different address than the one in her Articles of Organization, and that she filed under "Sherri's Grooming" rather than "Sherri's Grooming LLC." Her fix: refile her records with matching data, supply proof of local business license, and resubmit—this time, the account is approved.

Changing Details:

If you relocate or update your contact information, immediately update your records everywhere: the Secretary of State, the IRS (via Form 8822-B), your bank, state/local authorities, D&B, and all vendors. Set up a "business changes checklist" to avoid missing crucial updates.

Advanced Tip:

Keep a master spreadsheet (or secure digital folder) with *every* key piece of registration data—business address history, EIN, license numbers, contact points—so you can quickly resolve mismatches without digging through old emails or paperwork.

CHAPTER 2

COMPLIANCE AND CREDIBILITY SIGNALS

After establishing your LLC, the second bedrock of No-PG credit building is ongoing compliance and credibility. Here, details matter: tiny discrepancies in registration or expired documentation often explain why new businesses are denied or delayed.

Why Compliance Directly Impacts Credit Decisions

Modern lenders and underwriters increasingly rely on data automation. Their systems "scrape" public business databases, licensing registries, state/federal directories, and commercial websites. Any inconsistency—no matter how small—triggers a caution flag or denial. Conversely, perfect alignment signals you are a responsible, established operator.

Action Guidance

Regularly Review & Maintain Registrations, Licenses, and Permits

- Track renewal dates for every business registration (state, city, industry board).
- Set reminders to renew licenses at least 30–60 days before expiration.
- Keep up-to-date copies in a digital "compliance" folder. Missing or expired licenses can legally invalidate your business or block vendor/lender relationships.

Example:

A landscaping LLC in Ohio skips renewing its pesticide handler's license due to low winter sales. In spring, the owner applies for equipment financing; the reason for the denial? State license not active at time of application.

Match Business Records Exactly Across All Platforms

Compare every registration and public record for precision:

- Secretary of State articles
- IRS tax records
- All business bank accounts
- D&B and other credit bureau profiles
- Utility bills or lease agreements, if supporting docs are needed
- Standardize formatting (Ex, "123 Main Street" vs. "123 Main St.") and official spelling everywhere.

Mini Scenario:

Two business partners open "Creative Stack Studios, LLC" but are listed on the IRS EIN letter as "Creative Stack Studio LLC" (singular). This small error leads to months of vendor denials because they cannot reconcile the records.

Develop a Credible Online Presence

- A professional website and strong digital footprint signal seriousness.
- Include a clear business NAP (Name, Address, Phone) that matches your official filings.

- Secure recognizable domain-based email addresses (not Gmail/Yahoo), as many automated applications screen non-domain email as a fraud red flag.
- Update your Google Business Profile, Yelp, and other directories routinely to keep info up-to-date.

Example:

A supply vendor declines a new cleaning service. Upon appeal, the vendor credited the applicant for a well-designed website with matching company information, and approved a Net 30 account.

Establish a System for Reviewing Public Databases

- Regularly check your business listing in the Secretary of State database, D&B's D-U-N-S® search, and major online directories.
- Catch and fix errors before applications trigger problems.

Common Mistakes / Risk Awareness

- **Address/Name Inconsistencies:** Using abbreviations or alternate versions of your business name in various registrations leads to automated mismatches.
- **Expired Licensing:** Lenders may check professional/occupational licenses in public databases, and auto-reject expired records.

Edge Case:

A food service LLC in Florida applies for a Net 30 account during the annual health permit renewal season. Because the license status briefly switches to "pending," the vendor delays approval until the permit clears.

Troubleshooting / Recovery Guidance

Quarterly Compliance Audit:

Once a quarter, spend 30 minutes going through every database where your business is listed. Fix errors or request corrections—especially after any major business event (address change, ownership change, rebranding).

Attach Proof on Applications:

For sensitive applications, proactively upload or attach scans of your most current business license, formation certificate, and bank letter. This step can tip the scales in your favor for borderline cases and reduce processing delays.

Advanced Tip:

As you grow, designate a "compliance lead"—even if that's yourself—to handle annual/quarterly reviews, ensuring nothing slips through the cracks. Small teams sometimes delegate this to bookkeepers or outside advisors for extra peace of mind.

CHAPTER 3

UNDERSTANDING BUSINESS CREDIT REPORTING AND CYCLES

Business credit reports and scores are built on "tradelines"—accounts and payment histories reported to one or more business credit bureaus. However, the reporting landscape, especially with Dun & Bradstreet (D&B), is often confusing, with unpredictable time lags and inconsistent practices. Simply "opening accounts" does not guarantee that anything will appear on your credit profile.

Why Tradeline Reporting Isn't Instant

Bureaus like D&B, Experian, and Equifax Small Business process millions of vendor account updates, often relying on electronic file transfers and data feeds from major suppliers. Some vendors batch reports monthly, while others do so quarterly. Data is checked against your D-U-N-S® Number (D&B), EIN, and official business name/address for matching. Any mismatch causes a slowdown or outright omission.

Furthermore, some vendors require a minimum transaction size (e.g., $50 per invoice) *and* a positive payment history *before* they begin reporting.

Action Guidance

Get Your D-U-N-S® Number—Early

- D-U-N-S® Numbers are free from D&B and usually take up to 30 business days to process (rush service is available for a fee, but unnecessary in most cases).
- Vendors and lenders may auto-reject applicants if their D-U-N-S® Number cannot be validated.
- Register your D-U-N-S® profile with *identical* information to all other records.

Example:

Sarah forms her consulting LLC and waits 3 months before applying for a D-U-N-S® Number. Meanwhile, she opens two Net 30 accounts; when those vendors attempt to report, D&B has no profile to attach the tradelines—so the accounts are lost until she later re-applies and vendors re-report.

Understand Bureau Reporting Cycles

- D&B, like most bureaus, updates business files in cycles—monthly, bi-monthly, or even quarterly for some vendors.
- After you open and pay a Net 30 invoice, it typically takes 30–90 days for the tradeline to appear.
- Expect more delay in Q4 and Q1, when batches increase, or staff are reduced.
- Experian and Equifax Small Business can be faster or slower—there is no single industry standard.

Mini Scenario:

An LLC owner opens three Net 30 accounts in May, pays on time, but only sees one tradeline on her D&B report by July. The others show up in August and September, demonstrating how different vendors update at different rates.

What Bureaus Really Matter?

- **D&B:** Still the most referenced for trade and supplier credit decisions.

- **Experian Business:** Used by many major banks for credit cards and loans.
- **Equifax Small Business:** Gaining traction among credit card issuers and certain alternative lenders.
- Each bureau has its own scoring system (D&B's PAYDEX, Experian's Intelliscore, Equifax's Business Credit Risk Score).

Monitor Reports for Accuracy

- Use online credit monitoring—either directly through bureaus or via third-party platforms (Nav, CreditSignal, etc.).
- Check all details: company name, address, D-U-N-S® Number, tradeline count, payment history, and any derogatory marks.
- Monitor monthly during active credit-building (and at least quarterly ongoing).

Common Mistakes / Risk Awareness

- **Expecting Tradelines to Appear Instantly:** New tradelines often require 1–3 months to show—sometimes longer if a vendor has a batching backlog.

- **Assuming All Vendors Report:** Many vendors market "Net 30" terms, but fewer than half reliably report to business credit bureaus.
- **Failing to Monitor Reports:** Silence isn't golden. If you aren't actively inspecting your reports, you may accumulate missing tradelines or data errors that go undetected until you apply for more significant credit.

Advanced Decision Guidance

When choosing vendors, email or call ahead to confirm:

- To which bureau(s) will they report?
- What are the minimum order/payment requirements for a tradeline to be reported?
- How frequently do they send updates?

Troubleshooting / Recovery Guidance

Request Direct Reporting:

If a tradeline doesn't appear 60–90 days after payment, reach out to the vendor's credit or accounting department.

Politely request confirmation of their reporting process, providing your D-U-N-S® Number and detailed invoice/payment proof. In borderline cases, vendors may "force report" a missing account after manual review.

Check for Data Mismatches:

If a vendor says they've reported your tradeline, but it doesn't appear, examine the account for subtle differences in the listed business name, address, or EIN. Even a misplaced comma or abbreviating "LLC" can stall a connection at the bureau level.

Supporting Example: D&B Portal Walkthrough

Upon receiving a "notice of file update" from D&B, log in to your D&B portal. Under "Trade Payments," you find reporting from "ACME Office Supplies," but not your other vendor, "General Supply LLC."

Steps to diagnose:

- Review your profile's business name, address, and D-U-N-S® Number.
- Cross-reference that information with the exact details you used on the missing vendor's application and account.
- If any inconsistencies are found, contact "General Supply LLC" with the updated details, request they verify with D&B, and then follow up with D&B's support desk, providing a copy of your invoice and a note referencing your last payment.

Why This Process Can Fail

Vendor onboarding errors, outdated corporate data, or missed communication between staff and reporting systems often mean net 30 accounts aren't reported—even if you're told otherwise at the application phase. Persistence, documentation, and direct communication are vital to resolve these hiccups.

Chapter 4

Net 30 Vendor Accounts and Reporting Tradelines

Net 30 vendor accounts are designed to give new LLCs both operational flexibility and a real, reportable credit footprint. But their value hinges on proper selection, responsible usage, and diligent record-keeping.

How Net 30 Accounts Work (and Why They Matter)

A "Net 30" account allows you to order goods or services on credit, with thirty days to pay the invoice in full. When these accounts report to business credit bureaus, each on-time or early payment strengthens your business credit score and builds the foundation for No-PG approvals at higher tiers.

Variables Impacting Success

Not all vendor accounts are created equal. Variables to weigh include:

- *Reporting Consistency*: Does the vendor *always* report, or only if specific conditions are met?
- *Minimum Purchase*: Is a particular spend/deposit required to trigger a report?
- *Open to New Businesses*: Will the vendor grant net terms to an entity with 0–3 months' history, or only to those with established profiles?
- *Industry Sensitivity*: Do certain vendors screen out LLCs in "high risk" sectors, regardless of payment performance?

Action Guidance

Identify No-PG Vendors That Report

- Research and select 3–5 vendors widely acknowledged to report Net 30 accounts (examples: Uline, Quill, Grainger). Always verify at the time of application—vendor reporting policies may change without warning.
- If possible, search business credit forums for recent confirmation or call the vendor directly and request their reporting policy in writing.

Example 1:

Lily's new marketing LLC opens a Net 30 account with Uline, but only places a $30 order (below Uline's reporting threshold). Uline only reports invoices of $50 or more. Lily's first payment does not appear on her D&B profile, but her second (a $75 order) does.

Example 2:

Jamie applies to Grainger and is denied Net 30 terms as his company is only 21 days old. Grainger's underwriting system requires at least 30 days since state formation for consideration.

Apply Using Only Verified Business Info

- On vendor applications, list your correct LLC name, EIN, business address, and business phone. Do not use personal information or your social security number unless explicitly required—and only proceed if you can remain No-PG.
- If prompted, select "open account with EIN only" or respond as a business, not as an individual.

Make Qualifying Orders and Pay Promptly

- Place small, business-useful orders—office supplies, cleaning products, minor equipment.
- Aim to pay invoices before the Net 30 deadline. Early or on-time payments maximize the positive impact on the score. I recommend paying 7-10 days in advance of the due date.

Advanced Tip:

Some vendors will only start reporting after your second or third successful payment.

Scenario:

Sam's IT LLC places and pays for a $100 order with Quill, expecting immediate credit reporting. Quill's policy (as of this guide's writing) is to report only after the second order has been placed and paid. Sam learns to make a quick follow-up purchase to trigger reporting, and ensure his tradeline appears in the next cycle.

Keep Meticulous Documentation

- Save all order confirmations, invoices, payment receipts, and correspondence in both physical and digital form.

- Some bureaus or vendors may request detailed backup before researching a missing tradeline.
- Use a spreadsheet to track all application dates, order dates, payment dates, and reporting status.

Deeper Decision Guidance

Which Vendors to Prioritize?

Prioritize vendors who report to both D&B and Experian, as this covers more future lender requirements. If your industry is specialized (e.g., food service, trade work), seek suppliers who will offer Net 30 terms and are known to report, even if the minimum order size is higher.

When to Use Personal Guarantees?

Only provide an SSN if all other application options are exhausted *and* the application clearly indicates no personal credit pull or guarantee will result. Even then, ask the vendor for written clarification.

Common Mistakes / Risk Awareness

- **Non-Reporting Accounts:** Opening Net 30 accounts that make no report—even after months—wastes both your time and business spending.
- **Applying Prematurely:** Vendors often require you to be 30–60 days post-formation. Early applications get declined by a computer, sometimes without explanation. Due to automation denials, you should always try to contact the vendor support channels to clarify. I've had denials overturned by live operators.
- **Mixing Personal Data:** Using your own SSN or home address on business credit applications eliminates the business/personal separation you're working to establish.

Troubleshooting / Recovery Guidance

Vendor Denial Fix:

If denied, ask explicitly for the reason—age of business, data inconsistency, missing industry documentation, etc. Thank the account representative for their time, and ask for reconsideration after you correct the issue.

Example:

The new LLC was denied by Quill due to a mismatched address. The owner updates her official business address with the Secretary of State and IRS, re-applies, and this time is approved.

Missing Tradelines:

After making qualified purchases and paying promptly, wait up to 90 days before escalating. Then:

- Review all business records for matching details.
- Email the vendor's credit department: provide D-U-N-S® Number, invoice, and payment proof.
- If still unresolved, file a research request with the bureau (D&B or Experian), including documentation.

Supporting Example: Example Vendor Application

You decide to apply for a Net 30 account with Grainger:

- Register your company at Grainger.com under the business account portal, listing the LLC's full legal name, EIN, and business address.

- At checkout, opt for "Bill Me Net 30" terms, not "Pay Now" or individual credit options.
- Place a $60 order of facility maintenance supplies (above reporting threshold).
- On approval, pay the invoice promptly.
- After 45–75 days, check your D&B and Experian business credit reports for Grainger's tradeline.
- If it's missing, collect your order confirmation, payment receipt, and correspondence with Grainger; reach out to their credit department with a request to verify that your tradeline has been reported correctly, providing all necessary identifiers.

Advanced Tip:

Rotating vendors every few quarters—adding new ones known to report—can help maintain tradeline growth if certain accounts drop off (Ex, a supplier changes policy and stops reporting to D&B for new customers).

CHAPTER 5

BUILDING YOUR CREDIT PROFILE

Building business credit is a process of thoughtful progression, not shotgun application sprees. An intentional sequence increases your odds of approval, minimizes denials, and produces a stronger credit profile for future borrowing.

Why Sequencing Matters

Each new tradeline raises your business's credibility and signals responsible financial behavior. Sequential applications allow time for each tradeline to report, for scores to update, and for thin profiles to mature into robust ones. Rushing or batching applications, by contrast, can trigger mass denials, freeze reputational risk flags at bureaus, and leave your business "locked out" for a reporting cycle or longer.

Action Guidance

Map Your Approval Path

- Identify your first 3–5 initial reporting vendors, apply one at a time, and space out applications at least one week apart.
- After each successful account is opened and paid, await reporting confirmation before moving on. Use your tracking spreadsheet to momentum-build.

Example:

Alexa's LLC applies to Uline and is approved. She orders supplies and pays off her invoice. Three weeks later, she applies to Quill, repeating the process, and then to Grainger, ensuring that each vendor's reporting cycle is met in sequence.

Pause Between Credit Tiers

- Refrain from applying for Tier 2 credit (store, gas, or fleet cards) until 2–3 tradelines are visible on your business's D&B or Experian report.

- This deliberate staging not only reduces denials but raises your business's credit score more substantially.

Scenario:

A new LLC owner opens three Net 30 accounts and pays all invoices promptly, but immediately applies for a Lowe's card, a Shell fleet card, and an Office Depot card within a single week. Two are declined, one is "pending review". All cite missing tradelines or insufficient business credit in denial reasons.

Meticulously Document Each Step

- Log every application, account opening, invoice, payment, and confirmation of reporting in a business credit file. This log is your record for future lenders, and a powerful diagnostic if denials occur.

Advanced Tip:

Include the vendor, the bureau(s) reported to, the application date, the approval/denial date, the payment date, and the date the tradeline appeared on your report.

Periodically annotate with comments if delays or issues arise.

Build Gradually—Revisit Before You Apply Again

- Review your full progress before every new app: Are required tradelines reported? Are payments current? Are there any address/name/phone inconsistencies?
- Slow, steady application sequencing avoids unnecessary credit review "hard pulls" and allows you to spot and remedy mistakes before they compound.

Common Mistakes / Risk Awareness

- **Jumping Tiers Too Quickly:** Applying for fleet or store cards before your tradelines appear often triggers denial—sometimes even when you've paid invoices on time (due to bureau lags).
- **Batching or Mass Applying:** Multiple credit inquiries and applications in a short span can paint your LLC as high-risk or desperate, resulting in automated blocks and, potentially, a reputation freeze for months.

Troubleshooting / Recovery Guidance

- **If Denied Mid-Sequence:** Crosscheck every foundational step:
- Are all records current and consistent?
- Are you using the exact business name and address everywhere?
- Is your D-U-N-S® Number registered and active?
- Are previous vendor tradelines visible?
- Wait a full reporting cycle (30 days or more), remedy any issues, and only then reapply.
- If tradelines aren't reporting after 90 days despite correct payment, shift focus to another known reporting vendor and track closely.

Real-World Friction Point Example:

Maria, owner of a year-old LLC, received a denial for an Office Depot card after three vendor tradelines *were not* reported. On checking, only two are present—one vendor stopped reporting recently. By rotating to another vendor and waiting for the cycle to complete, Maria reapplies and is approved.

Advanced Tip:

Every few months, consult current business credit-building forums or reputable advisor sites for live updates on which vendors are actively reporting. Business credit reporting is a dynamic environment; staying informed keeps your sequencing strategy effective.

CHAPTER 6

VERIFYING AND MONITORING PROGRESS

Verifying what your business credit reports *actually* say—versus what you expect or have been told—is as important as paying vendors on time. Building and maintaining a functional business credit file requires vigilance, accurate self-audits, and a quick response to reporting failures.

Why Monthly Monitoring Protects Your Progress

Errors, omissions, and vendor mistakes are common at all stages. Sometimes vendors pause reporting due to system updates, data mismatches cause lost tradelines, or bureau glitches drop or mislabel your account information. If left undetected and unfixed, these small issues can undermine months of careful building.

Action Guidance

Schedule Structured, Monthly Credit Checks

- Use a recurring reminder to log in to each major bureau (D&B, Experian Business, Equifax Small Business) and inspect your business's credit file.
- Review for:
- New or missing tradelines
- Payment status accuracy (are all payments recorded as "current" or "on time"?)
- Score updates or alerts for derogatory information, collection entries, or disputes

Example:

On a monthly review, you see that your Quill tradeline is present on D&B but missing from Experian. On checking Quill's current policy (as of your application), you realize Experian reporting requires a second qualifying transaction—so you plan accordingly.

Manually Verify All Account Details

- Each account, invoice, and payment entry should align with your LLC's legal name, address, and D-U-N-S® Number. A mismatch may result in tradelines being "orphaned"—reported, but not matched to your file.
- Use cross-referenced spreadsheets/logs to flag differences.

Proactively Address Missing or Inaccurate Tradelines

- If a tradeline is missing 30–60 days post-payment, contact the vendor's credit or reporting team, requesting a confirmation of the report and the information under which it was submitted.
- If it's still missing or mis-reported, reach out to the credit bureau's support to request an investigation—include all documentation, D-U-N-S® Number, application confirmation, invoice, and proof of payment.

Scenario:

Anthony's Catering, LLC account with a supply company is not listed under his business name on D&B. After investigation, he learns the account was set up under "Tony's Catering, LLC" instead of "Anthony's Catering, LLC". With documentation, D&B amends his file.

Archive Screenshots and Paper Trails

- Take regular screenshots of your tradelines as proof of reporting. This is valuable evidence for lenders wary of thin files or for filing disputes if details are lost during a bureau operating system update.
- Store all records—application, approval email, invoice, payment proof, and report screenshot—in a secure, organized folder.

Common Mistakes / Risk Awareness

- **Counting on Automatic, Continuous Vendor Reporting:** Some vendors periodically drop reporting, especially after changing credit policies, switching bureaus, or updating computer systems.

- **Ignoring Minor Data Discrepancies:** Even a minor address typo or name variant can block or redirect a tradeline.

Troubleshooting / Recovery Guidance

If Vendor Claims to Report, But No Bureau Data Appears:

- Double-check every submitted detail.
- Forward all proof to both the vendor and credit bureau, requesting a manual match or investigation.
- Rotate in another vendor if reporting failure persists, especially after 90 days.

If Incorrect Tradeline Data or Payments Are Reported:

- File a correction/dispute with the credit bureau (each has online or mail-based dispute channels).
- Provide backup documentation: invoices, payment confirmations, correspondence, license, and EIN documentation.

Advanced Tip:

Consider using reputable business credit applications (Ex, Nav) linked to the major bureaus—these can offer aggregated alerts, score tracking, and sometimes automatic reporting "boosts" through account connections.

For 24/7 monitoring of your business credit profile across all three bureaus, I use and recommend NAV — one of the most trusted tools available for small business owners.

Scan this QR code to learn more.

Or type this URL in your browser

https://www.pantheonspace.com/nav

Mini-Case Study:

Correcting Reporting Errors. After observing a sudden, mysterious decline in Brian's business credit score, I conducted a thorough review of his report. Quickly discovered a late payment entry from an unfamiliar vendor. A clear reporting error.

By proactively reaching out to the credit bureau and submitting evidence that the account did not match his EIN, business address, or records, we successfully had the negative record removed. Then, the score was restored, allowing him to secure approval for his Tier 2 credit application.

CHAPTER 7

ADVANCING TO FLEET CARDS AND STORE CREDIT

Transitioning from basic vendor accounts to practical, No-PG "real world" credit options—such as fleet, gas, and store cards—is a significant milestone in establishing business credit. However, trying to advance too quickly or with an insufficient profile is a common pitfall for many entrepreneurs.

What Tier 2 Credit Involves

Tier 2 credit includes store credit for major chains such as Office Depot, Lowe's, and Staples. It also includes fuel and fleet cards, such as Shell or WEX, and, in some cases, business-issued charge cards.

These products require two things before you can access them: established tradelines and a demonstrated history of responsible payments. Most offer No-PG pathways — meaning no personal guarantee required — but policies shift frequently. Economic downturns and tighter lender scrutiny can quickly change the rules.

Always verify current terms before applying.

Action Guidance

Identify and Verify Tier 2 Credit Sources

- Before applying, confirm:
- How many positive tradelines are required for standard approval (for many, 3 is the minimum; some require 5)
- Their precise "No-PG" policy—call and request written guidelines, if possible
- Which bureaus do they pull and report to
- Choose products serving your core business needs and match your typical spending.

Example:

A construction LLC selects Lowe's and Shell Fleet cards, both of which (on last policy review) offer EIN-only applications and regularly report to D&B and Experian Business.

Verify Tradeline Status Before Any Application

- Log in to D&B and Experian to confirm that at least three active, on-time tradelines exist.

- Print or save this as "application proof". Especially if high-value or urgent purchases are planned.

Scenario:

Diane's Bakery LLC wants an Office Depot credit card. She checks her report and notes that only two tradelines are present; she waits another reporting cycle after adding a third vendor, then applies and is approved.

Apply Without a Personal Guarantee

- Select the "business account" or "EIN-only" route explicitly. If online applications require a SSN or personal guarantee, pause the process and call to confirm whether a paper or alternate app is available.
- Ensure all business data matches credit files perfectly.

Edge Case:

A supplier's online application has a required field for a gas card. You now have a prompt to enter a SSN, but the instructions at the bottom say, "Call our credit team for EIN-only application process."

The applicant calls, receives a PDF, and applies using only business credentials, protecting their personal credit.

Utilize and Repay Responsibly

- Use approved accounts for ordinary, recurring business expenses.
- Pay balances in full every cycle. A late payment on a Tier 2 account can irreparably damage your growing business credit.
- Maintain low utilization to avoid appearing overextended.

Deeper Decision Guidance

Should You Apply for Maximum Limits?

Only request limits and products in line with your current revenues and purchasing needs. Applying for "aspirational" high limits may prompt denials or manual file reviews requiring more time in business or documented revenue.

When to Move Beyond Tier 2?

Only after 6+ months of flawless payment history, with 5+ positive tradelines.

And documented, rising business revenue. Then you can consider advanced No-PG credit (like bank lines or unsecured term loans).

Common Mistakes / Risk Awareness

- **Assuming No-PG Status is Permanent:** Even "guaranteed" No-PG accounts may switch policies—especially after economic downturns or fraud spikes. Always confirm the latest terms prior to submitting applications.
- **Overapplying/Overextending Credit:** Opening multiple high-limit accounts without business need or adequate revenue signals risk to underwriters.

Troubleshooting / Recovery Guidance

SSN or PG Suddenly Required:

If you hit an SSN or PG roadblock mid-application, do not proceed or "test the waters". This may trigger a hard inquiry or link your personal credit for the life of the account. Instead, call the issuer, request the EIN-only application, or wait for policy updates.

If Denied:

Reach out to the credit issuer's business division, requesting a written explanation. Ask specifically:

- Was a lack of tradelines the problem?
- Was business age or revenue referenced?
- Were there any issues with business data (address inconsistency, incomplete licensing)?
- Fix what you can, then calendar a re-application window based on issuer recommendations.

Advanced Tip:

Set up a recurring "policy review" for your short list of desired cards. Vendor and fleet card policies can shift quarterly. Subscribing to key lenders' business credit newsletters or checking authoritative small business forums keeps you well ahead of sudden changes.

CHAPTER 8

TIMING TERM LOANS AND HIGHER LIMITS

As your business matures, the most sought-after No-PG credit products require demonstrated performance: time in business, visible revenue, and financial operations that reflect solid management. Now your mindset and bookkeeping must transition from “startup step” to “serious operator.”

Understanding When Banks and Lenders Shift Their Evaluation

While many vendor, store, or fleet accounts can be opened with a clean business record and three tradelines alone, true lines of credit, working capital loans, or card products with $25k+ limits require two additional elements:

- *Time*: Most reputable banks/issuers won’t approve major No-PG products for businesses with less than one to two years of operating history.
- *Revenue*: Many now require proof of annualized revenue—commonly $100k–$250k+ for significant credit lines.

Action Guidance

Recognize These Lender Thresholds, Not Just Rules of Thumb

- Macroeconomic trends influence lenders' underwriting practices. The revenue and time requirements adjust as fraud risk or default rates rise and fall.
- Research targeted lenders' or issuers' *posted* requirements (if available); when in doubt, call the small business credit department and request confirmation.

Example:

A vending machine LLC applies for a $50,000 business credit card six months after launch, submits solid tradelines, but only $50,000 in annualized revenue. The application is denied for "insufficient business history and revenue." The business owner requests details, learns $100,000 is the minimum, and focuses on additional growth before reapplying.

Document and Present Financials Professionally

- Prepare six months' or more of clean business bank statements. These are usually the first financials requested for No-PG reviews at banks and advanced lenders.
- Compile, or have your accountant/bookkeeper compile, a simple profit & loss (P&L) statement and basic balance sheet.
- Automation tools (QuickBooks, FreshBooks, Wave, etc.) can streamline this; for microbusinesses, Basic Excel sheets tracking revenue and expenses suffice as long as they are accurate.

Scenario:

Jen's marketing agency makes $12,000 per month. She's able to show six months of increasing revenue, current vendor and store tradelines, and a simple cash flow chart. She applies for a $25,000 business line of credit. While this does not guarantee approval, her documentation meets the lender's published standards and secures a manual review rather than an instant rejection.

Time Bigger Moves for When You Genuinely Qualify

- Only apply for bank loans, higher credit limits, or No-PG term products after clear, lender-confirmed eligibility (age and revenue).
- Be honest with yourself about weaknesses. If your revenue is lumpy or negative, pause and shore up your finances.

Common Mistakes / Risk Awareness

Applying Far Too Soon:

Repeated application attempts before eligibility can "lock out" your business file and flag you to compliance teams. That will create bureaucratic hurdles and slower processing for future, properly sequenced applications.

Fudging Revenue or "Estimates":

Supply only fully verifiable, true financials. "Pro-forma" (projected) numbers are rarely accepted, and overstatement is a compliance risk. If caught, you may be blacklisted by bureaus or lenders.

Troubleshooting / Recovery Guidance

- **If Denied, Request Clarity:** Don't guess. Contact the lender for a plain-English explanation.

Example questions:

- "What is the current minimum revenue/time in business for this product?"
- "If I meet these criteria in six months, will prior applications count against me?"
- Record the answers and use them to plan your next steps.

Strengthen Where Possible:

- Increase monthly deposits by prioritizing business sales/payments.
- Replace non-reporting vendors and add additional tradelines as supporting evidence of responsibility.
- Always keep payments current. Late payments or bounced checks can tank your case for higher limits.

Advanced Tip:

Some lenders offer "pre-qualification checks" that will not affect your credit profile. Use these to gauge approval odds and identify weak spots without risking hard inquiries or denials on your formal bureau record.

Mini-Case:

Tom, owner of an equipment rental LLC, is denied a $30,000 business credit card. The lender's adverse action notice cites "insufficient time in business (4 months)" and "annual gross revenue below program minimum." Tom waits until month 12, increases business bank account activity past $120k annualized, and is successful on his second application.

CHAPTER 9

FRICTION, DENIAL, AND RECOVERY STEPS

Even the best-prepared businesses encounter application denials, bureaucratic friction, or reporting failures. As a responsible operator, your strategy for these moments determines your long-term credibility and success. Ethical conduct is not just the right thing to do, it is the key to sustainable, scalable business credit.

Diagnosing Why Denials Happen

No-PG lenders and bureaus use both automated and human review processes, scrutinizing every detail for fraud, non-compliance, or inexperience. Denials often cite "insufficient history," "unverifiable information," or "data mismatch". Diagnose these with surgical precision.

Action Guidance

Confirm a Pre-Application Checklist Before Every Submission

- Legal business name/address match on ALL records

- Up-to-date licenses and registrations
- Minimum required tradelines reporting, per the target card/vendor
- Zero open delinquencies or unresolved disputes

Advanced Tip:

Keep your pre-application checklist on your desktop or team workspace. Use it every time, no matter how obvious the details feel.

Track Every Denial and Friction Event

- Document denial letters, emails, or portal messages. Note the contact, time, and stated or implied reason.
- Create columns in your spreadsheet for "Denial Reason" and "Corrective Action." Repeat issues become trends and deserve deeper investigation.

Scenario:

Brianna's Auto Detailing LLC is repeatedly denied by vendors for "unverifiable business address." Her log shows she used a "suite" in one entry and "#200" in another. The mismatch, once corrected, resolves future denials.

Learn From Every Denial

- Every denial contains at least one fixable detail. Categorize responses:
- **Fix Now:** Address mismatch, missing license, old EIN, insufficient tradelines present, spelling errors.
- **Requires Time:** Business must season; more revenue needed; more payment history required.

Common Mistakes / Risk Awareness

- **Immediate Reapplying:** Submitting the same or similar application without changing a thing is usually flagged as "system gaming" and can slow future reviews.
- **Taking Bad Shortcuts:** Engaging in "credit builder" packages that promise tradelines for a fee or using fake references presents long-term risks—denial, blacklisting, and, in rare cases, referral for regulatory review.

Troubleshooting / Recovery Guidance

Repeated Denials:

- Stop all new applications for 30+ days.

- Analyze every foundational component—addresses, names, numbers, registration dates, tradeline ages.
- If you cannot isolate the cause, book a consultation with a business compliance specialist or CPA with business credit experience.
- Update your strategy: rotate in new, confirmed-reporting vendors, or space new applications one per month after a reporting cycle.

Longstanding Reporting Failures:

- Track the last *successful* report for each vendor. If a vendor has stopped reporting, research current policy or call directly.
- Proactively "retire" non-reporting vendors and replace with newer accounts.

Supporting Example: Annotated Denial Letter

- "Dear Applicant,
- After review, we were unable to approve your business credit application for the following reason(s):
- Insufficient trade payment history reported;
- Business address did not match registration file.

- You are welcome to reapply once these issues are resolved."

Analysis:

- "Insufficient trade payment history" = Not enough vendor tradelines reporting to the credit bureau.
- "Business address did not match registration file" = Your Secretary of State or IRS file doesn't match the address you used on the application.

Repair Steps:

- Log in to your credit bureau portals and count the actual tradelines showing.
- Audit every public business record. Update addresses at the Secretary of State, IRS (Form 8822-B), D&B, etc.
- Wait for updates to propagate and for new tradelines to be reported (often a 30+ day process).
- Only then, reapply with confidence.

Advanced Tip:

If your industry regularly experiences denials due to "high risk" labels, document each denial and escalate them to both the vendor and, if policy-driven, your local chamber of commerce or trade group. Sometimes, policy exceptions or new vendor relationships can be brokered through industry-specific networking.

Ethical Operator Guidance

No matter how frustrating denials may be, resist all temptations to manufacture history, create "phantom" tradelines, or pay for unauthorized reference services. The risks of legal, reputational, and financial harm far outweigh any potential short-term benefit.

CONCLUSION

Practical Next Steps

Set Up a Monthly Review Schedule:

Block off one hour every month for credit report audits, documentation checks, and follow-ups on unresolved vendor or bureau issues.

Apply for New Credit Only When Ready:

Once you have tradelines reporting and your business has the required age and/or revenue, apply mindfully for only the products you genuinely need.

Monitor Industry and Vendor Policy Shifts:

Add a recurring item to verify that target vendors and cards still offer No-PG, EIN-only routes, and active bureau reporting.

Reinforce Reader Confidence and Competence

You are pursuing business credit through the highest ethical and professional standards. This path is not the fast lane. It's the smart, sustainable road. Every time a vendor reports a payment, every time a tradeline populates, and every time a responsible account brings you closer to the legitimacy, flexibility, and resilience that small business operators require.

Real-world credit building rarely happens on a schedule. Denials, delays, and policy changes will arise. Stay the course.

Use checklists, investigate every friction point, and never lose sight of your data accuracy or compliance. With discipline, patience, and steady documentation, your LLC will stand apart from the crowd—ready for funding, growth, and opportunity, all while keeping your personal credit and assets protected.

Above all: Stay ethical. Stay accurate. Stay persistent.

Business credit is a marathon, not a sprint. If you lay a solid foundation, you'll never need shortcuts.

The First 90 Days

This checklist is also available as a free digital download — fillable on any device or printable on standard 8.5 x 11 paper. Or feel free to write your answers directly in this book.

Scan the QR code or visit **pantheonspace.com/90daystocredit** to get your free copy.

FIRST 90 DAYS
COMPLIANCE CHECKLIST

Your Step-by-Step Foundation for Business Credit Readiness

This checklist walks you through every task you need to complete in your first 90 days of business credit building — in the correct order, at the correct time. Do not skip steps. Do not rush phases. Each phase builds on the one before it.

Tip: Keep this checklist in a folder with your EIN confirmation, Articles of Organization, and bank account documents. You will reference these repeatedly.

This checklist belongs to:

____

Name / LLC Name

______________________________ ______________________________

Date Started *Day 90 Target Date*

PHASE 1 | DAYS 1–30 | Build Your Legal Foundation

> *Phase Goal: Get your LLC properly formed, registered, and documented so that every future credit application starts from a position of legitimacy. Every item in this phase must match every other item — exactly, every time.*

Register Your LLC Properly

- ☐ File your Articles of Organization with your state's Secretary of State office
- ☐ Specify your business name, address, registered agent, and ownership structure in the filing
- ☐ Keep the official filed copy in a safe place — you will need it repeatedly
- ☐ Establish your exact legal business name — including punctuation and 'LLC' — and use it consistently everywhere forever

My exact legal business name: ______________________________

State of formation: ______________________________

Date filed: ______________________________

Filing confirmation number: ______________________________

> *'Main Street LLC' and 'Main Street, LLC' are different names to a bureau. Use your exact legal name every single time — no variations.*

Example: You form 'Mason Creek Logistics LLC' but your bank lists you as 'Mason Creek Logistics' (without LLC) and a vendor spells it 'Mason Creek Logistics, LLC.' These variations cause reporting mismatches and, in the worst cases, outright denials.

Obtain Your EIN from the IRS

- ☐ Apply at IRS.gov — it is free, and approval is often immediate
- ☐ Store your EIN confirmation notice safely — you will need it for banks, vendors, and credit agencies

My EIN: ______________________

Date obtained: ______________________

☐ *Confirmation letter saved: ☐ Yes*

Example: An LLC owner delays applying for an EIN and tries to use their SSN instead. This links all 'business credit' activity to their personal record — not the LLC — permanently undermining the separation they are working to build.

Open a Dedicated Business Checking Account

- ☐ Open a business checking account using your exact LLC legal name and EIN only
- ☐ Never use your personal account for business transactions — commingling funds risks your liability protections
- ☐ Research banks in your area — not all are business-friendly for new entities
- ☐ Have ready: Articles of Organization, EIN, valid ID, and business license if required locally

Bank name: ______________________

Account opened: ______________________

☐ *Account uses exact LLC name: ☐ Yes*

Set Up Your Business Address and Phone Number

- ☐ Establish a dedicated business address — residential addresses and mailbox-only stores can be flagged by automated systems
- ☐ Consider a commercial mailing address or co-working space — avoid UPS Store-style mailboxes, many lenders have blacklisted these
- ☐ Secure a dedicated business phone number under your LLC name — not your personal cell
- ☐ Purchase a business domain and create a professional email using that domain

Business address: ______________________

Business phone: ______________________

Business domain: ______________________

Business email: ______________________

List Your Business with 411 Directory Assistance

- ☐ Register your business name and phone number with 411 directory assistance
- ☐ Some legacy lenders still reference this to verify legitimacy — it takes minutes and adds a credibility signal

411 listing confirmed:
☐ Yes Date: ______________________

Register for Your D-U-N-S® Number

- ☐ Go to Dun & Bradstreet's website and register for your free D-U-N-S® Number
- ☐ Use the exact same business name, address, and contact information as your LLC formation documents
- ☐ Processing takes up to 30 business days — register immediately, do not wait
- ☐ Vendors and lenders may auto-reject applicants if their D-U-N-S® Number cannot be validated

D-U-N-S® registration submitted: ☐ **Yes**
Date: ______________________

Expected confirmation date: ______________________

PHASE COMPLETE? Confirm all items before proceeding.
☐ Every item in Phase 1 is checked
☐ My business name is identical across ALL registrations
☐ My business address is identical across ALL registrations
☐ My EIN confirmation letter is saved and accessible
☐ My D-U-N-S® Number registration is submitted and processing
☐ Do NOT advance to Phase 2 until every item above is confirmed

PHASE 2 | DAYS 31–60 | Establish Your Credit Identity

Phase Goal: Make your business visible and verifiable to credit bureaus and vendors before you apply for anything. Visibility comes before credit. You cannot build what bureaus cannot see.

Confirm Your D-U-N-S® Number

- ☐ Log in to Dun & Bradstreet and confirm your D-U-N-S® Number has been issued and your profile is active
- ☐ Verify that your business name, address, and phone number match your formation documents exactly
- ☐ Correct any discrepancies immediately before any vendor applications

D-U-N-S® Number confirmed: ______________________________

☐ *Profile verified and accurate: ☐ Yes*

Any discrepancies found and corrected: ______________________________

Cross-Check All Records for Exact Consistency

Compare every registration and public record side by side. Do not assume they match — look them up and confirm.

Record Source	Business Name (exact)	Business Address (exact)	Business Phone (exact)
Secretary of State			
IRS Records			
Business Bank Account			
D&B Profile			
All Vendor Accounts			
Website / Directory			

☐ All records match exactly: ☐ Yes

Discrepancies found and corrected: ________________________________

Set Up Your Google Business Profile

- ☐ Create or claim your Google Business Profile using your exact business name, address, and phone number
- ☐ Verify your profile matches all other registrations exactly — same name, address, and phone
- ☐ This increases your digital credibility and helps vendors verify your legitimacy during application reviews

  - ☐ *Google Business Profile created: ☐ Yes*
  - ☐ *Information matches all other records exactly: ☐ Yes*

Open a Bureau Monitoring Account

- ☐ Set up monitoring for your business credit profile before applying for any vendor accounts
- ☐ Nav.com is a reliable starting point — it aggregates data from D&B, Experian, and Equifax in one dashboard
- ☐ You need to see what bureaus see before vendors do

Monitoring account set up at: ______________________________

Date activated: ______________________________

Apply for Your First Net 30 Vendor Account

- ☐ Select your first vendor — choose one that reports to D&B or Experian and does not require a personal guarantee
- ☐ Apply using only your business name, EIN, business address, and business phone — never your SSN unless confirmed No-PG in writing
- ☐ Place a qualifying order above the vendor's minimum reporting threshold
- ☐ Pay the invoice 7-10 days before the Net 30 deadline — early payment maximizes score impact

Vendor applied to: ________________________

Date applied: ________________________

Result: ☐ Approved
☐ Pending
☐ Denied

Order amount: ________________________

Invoice due date: ________________________

Date paid early: ________________________

> *If denied — do not reapply immediately. Record the denial reason, correct the issue, and wait at least 7 days before reapplying. Every denial has a fixable cause.*

Start Your Tradeline Tracking Log

- ☐ Open your Tradeline Reporting Verification Log and enter your first vendor account
- ☐ Record: application date, approval date, order date, payment date, and expected reporting date
- ☐ Update it every time anything changes — this log is your paper trail and diagnostic tool

☐ *Tracking log started: ☐ Yes*

PHASE COMPLETE? Confirm all items before proceeding.
☐ D-U-N-S® Number confirmed and profile verified
☐ All records cross-checked and consistent across all platforms
☐ Google Business Profile live and accurate
☐ Bureau monitoring account active
☐ First vendor account applied for
☐ First qualifying order placed and paid early
☐ Tradeline tracker started
☐ Do NOT advance to Phase 3 until every item above is confirmed

PHASE 3 | DAYS 61–90 | Activate, Verify, and Advance

Phase Goal: Confirm your tradelines are reporting, identify any gaps, complete your second and third vendor applications, and assess your readiness for Tier 2 credit. This phase is about verification and expansion — not rushing.

Check Your First Bureau Credit Report

- ☐ Log in to your bureau monitoring account and pull your D&B and Experian Business reports
- ☐ Note your current tradeline count and PAYDEX score if available
- ☐ Note any data discrepancies — wrong business name, address, or account details
- ☐ Screenshot and save everything

Date of first report check: ______________________

D&B PAYDEX Score (if available): ______________________

Tradelines visible on D&B: ______________________

Tradelines visible on Experian: ______________________

Any discrepancies noted: ______________________

Verify Your First Tradeline Is Reporting

- ☐ Confirm your first vendor account appears on your D&B or Experian report
- ☐ If it does not appear within 60-90 days of payment — contact the vendor's credit department and request confirmation of reporting
- ☐ Provide your D-U-N-S® Number and detailed invoice and payment proof when following up

☐ *Tradeline appeared on report: ☐ Yes ☐ Not yet — follow up initiated*

Bureau it appeared on: ______________________________

Date appeared: ______________________________

Example: If a vendor confirms they reported your tradeline but it doesn't appear — check whether the business name, address, or EIN submitted matches your bureau profile exactly. Even a misplaced comma can prevent a match.

Apply for Second Net 30 Vendor Account

- ☐ Once your first vendor is confirmed and paid — apply for your second vendor
- ☐ Space applications at least 7 days apart — never apply to two vendors in the same week
- ☐ Use the same EIN-only process and track everything in your verification log

Second vendor applied to: ______________________

Date applied: ______________________

Result:
☐ Approved
☐ Pending
☐ Denied

Order amount: ______________________

Date paid early: ______________________

Apply for Third Net 30 Vendor Account

- ☐ After your second vendor is confirmed and an order placed — apply for your third
- ☐ Three active, reporting tradelines is your minimum threshold for Tier 2 credit consideration

Third vendor applied to: ______________________

Date applied: ______________________

Result: ☐ Approved ☐ Pending ☐ Denied ______________________

Order amount: ______________________

Date paid early: ______________________

Complete a Full Records Consistency Audit

- ☐ Go through every database where your business is listed and confirm name, address, and phone are identical everywhere
- ☐ Fix any discrepancies immediately — even a minor address difference can block or redirect a tradeline
- ☐ Check: Secretary of State, IRS, bank, D&B, Experian, all vendors, Google, 411

☐ *Audit completed: ☐ Yes Date:* ____________

Discrepancies found and corrected: ______________________

Complete Your Tier 2 Readiness Assessment

Answer every condition honestly before applying for any Tier 2 credit — store cards, fleet cards, or gas cards.

Tier 2 Readiness Condition	☐
I have at least 3 active tradelines visible on my D&B or Experian Business report	☐
All tradelines show on-time or early payment status	☐
My LLC has been operating for a minimum of 60-90 days	☐
My business records — name, address, phone, EIN — are consistent everywhere	☐
My D-U-N-S® Number is active, verified, and matches all other records	☐

All five checked? ☐ Yes — you are ready to consider Tier 2 applications.

Any unchecked? Stop — resolve them before applying. A premature Tier 2 application does more damage than waiting another 30 days.

PHASE COMPLETE? Confirm all items before proceeding.
☐ First bureau report checked and saved
☐ First tradeline verified as reporting on at least one bureau
☐ Second vendor applied for, order placed, invoice paid early
☐ Third vendor applied for, order placed, invoice paid early
☐ Full records consistency audit completed
☐ Tier 2 Readiness Assessment completed
☐ Tradeline Reporting Verification Log fully updated

QUICK REFERENCE — MOST COMMON MISTAKES TO AVOID

⚠ Name inconsistency

'Main Street LLC' and 'Main Street, LLC' are different to a bureau. Use your exact legal name — every time, without exception.

⚠ Rushing Phase 2

Applying for vendors before your D-U-N-S® Number is confirmed means tradelines have nowhere to attach. Wait for confirmation.

⚠ Using personal information

Your SSN on a vendor application links that account to your personal credit permanently. Always use EIN only unless No-PG is confirmed in writing.

⚠ Ignoring denials

Every denial has a fixable cause. Diagnose before reapplying — submitting the same information to the same vendor gets the same result.

⚠ Not monitoring reports

If you aren't checking your bureau reports regularly you won't catch reporting failures until they cost you an application.

⚠ Rushing Tier 2

Applying for Tier 2 credit before three tradelines are confirmed on your bureau report is the single most common — and most expensive — mistake.

KEY RESOURCES

IRS EIN Application	*irs.gov/businesses/small-businesses-self-employed/apply-for-an-employer-identification-number-ein-online*
D-U-N-S® Number Registration	*dnb.com/duns-number.html*
D&B Credit Monitor	*app.dnb.com*
Experian Business	*experian.com/business*
Equifax Small Business	*equifax.com/business/small-business*
Nav — Business Credit Monitoring	*nav.com*
Secretary of State Finder	*sos.state.[yourstate].us*

This checklist is part of the Pantheon Space Academy Business Credit Starter Kit.

pantheonspace.com

Resources

This section offers credible starting points for further learning and independent verification of the business credit concepts covered in this guide. Because requirements, vendor reporting practices, and compliance standards can evolve, readers are encouraged to consult these recognized organizations directly for the most up-to-date guidance.

How to use these notes

- Use these links to verify specifics about business registration, EINs, credit bureau profiles, and reporting cycles.
- Search each site for policy updates, application instructions, or dispute processes relevant to your situation.
- Consult official business and credit glossaries for clear definitions of terms (e.g., 'No-PG', 'tradeline').
- Look up how to correct or update business information at credit bureaus or with government entities.

- Check for sample compliance checklists, forms, and common denial reasons straight from the primary source.
- Review official FAQs or support sections for troubleshooting reporting or profile visibility issues.
- Use contact/support sections on organization sites to get direct assistance with unresolved concerns.

Sources

- **LLC business identity / state filings** (Government)
    - U.S. Small Business Administration (SBA)
    - https://sba.gov
- **Employer Identification Number (EIN) application and guides** (Government)
    - Internal Revenue Service (IRS)
    - https://irs.gov
- **Business credit basics & compliance checklists** (Government)
    - U.S. Small Business Administration (SBA)
    - https://sba.gov/business-guide/manage-your-business/business-credit

- **Business credit bureau profiles & D-U-N-S® Number** (Public Institution)
    - Dun & Bradstreet
    - https://dnb.com
- **Business credit file / tradeline questions** (Public Institution)
    - Experian Business
    - https://experian.com/business
- **Small business credit reporting overview** (Public Institution)
    - Equifax Small Business
    - https://equifax.com/business/small-business
- **How business credit scores are calculated (Paydex, Intelliscore, etc.)** (Government)
    - U.S. Small Business Administration (SBA)
    - https://sba.gov/business-guide/manage-your-business/business-credit-scores
- **Business banking account requirements** (Government)
    - Federal Deposit Insurance Corporation (FDIC)
    - https://fdic.gov

- **Credit reporting standards and dispute rights** (Government)
    - Consumer Financial Protection Bureau (CFPB)
    - https://consumerfinance.gov
- **Business credit report monitoring and verification tools** (Public Institution)
    - NAV
    - https://nav.com
- **Business information listings and verification (411 directory, business phone)** (Government)
    - Federal Communications Commission (FCC)
    - https://fcc.gov
- **General standards for data matching and business identity accuracy** (Standards)
    - National Institute of Standards and Technology (NIST)
    - https://nist.gov
- **Reporting cycles, tradeline verification, and corrections** (Public Institution)
    - Dun & Bradstreet Help Center
    - https://dnb.com/utility-pages/support.html

- **Business credit card and loan requirements** (Government)
    - Federal Reserve
    - https://federalreserve.gov
- **Legal separation of business and personal credit** (Professional Association)
    - American Bar Association (ABA)
    - https://americanbar.org
- **Small business risk management, scams, and compliance safety** (Government)
    - Federal Trade Commission (FTC)
    - https://ftc.gov

Note

This appendix is provided for educational purposes only. Readers should always confirm current requirements, policies, and reporting practices directly with the official organizations or bureaus before making credit decisions.

www.ingramcontent.com/pod-product-compliance
Lightning Source LLC
Chambersburg PA
CBHW041302210926
51847CB00010B/120
* 9 7 8 1 9 7 0 9 6 5 0 0 1 *